HOW TO CLOSE MORE SALES TOI TOMORROW AND FOREVER

A REPEATABLE SYSTEM THAT GUARANTEES GREAT RESULTS

By Thomas Ellis

Legal Disclaimer:

While all attempts have been made to verify information provided in this e-book, the author does not assume any responsibility for errors, omissions, or contrary interpretation covered on this subject matter herein.

This publication is not intended for use as a source of legal or accounting advice. The author wants to state that information contained herein may be subject to varying state and/or local laws and regulations.

The reader of this e-book assumes all responsibility for the use of all of the contained material and information. Always adhere to all applicable laws, regulations, governering professional licensing, business tactics, and advertising. The reader/purchaser must also follow any local, state, or federal laws dealing with all aspects of business in the United States or abroad. This is the sole responsibility of the reader/purchaser of this e-book.

You can get anything you want in life if you just help enough other people get what they want.

Zig Ziglar

Table of Contents

The Art of Selling Introduction 5

What is Prospecting? 6

10 Tips for Successful Prospecting..7

Targeting Your Audience 9

Strategies/Methods on Getting Face to Face Meetings 9

First Appointment Strategy 12

Close for the Next Step 14

Closing More Sales Today 16

Getting Prospects Excited About Doing Business with You 17

Final Thoughts 20

ABOUT THE AUTHOR 21

The Art of Selling Introduction

The inspiration for writing this book comes from all the sales professionals I have managed and coached over the last 30 years. I realized that many things have changed regarding how buyers make decisions on what they purchase and who they purchase from. The fact remains, that the selling process has not changed.

Throughout this book I want to emphasize that, whether you are a business owner looking to increase your sales revenues or you are employed as a sales representative for a company with a sales quota, the sales process should be easy and simple to implement.

At the end of the day, people buy from people that they like, trust and who add significant value. Your job is to help people exceed the goals that they desire. When you are able to do this on a consistent basis, you will close more business than you could ever dream of.

You can get anything you want in life if you just help enough other people get what they want – Zig Ziglar

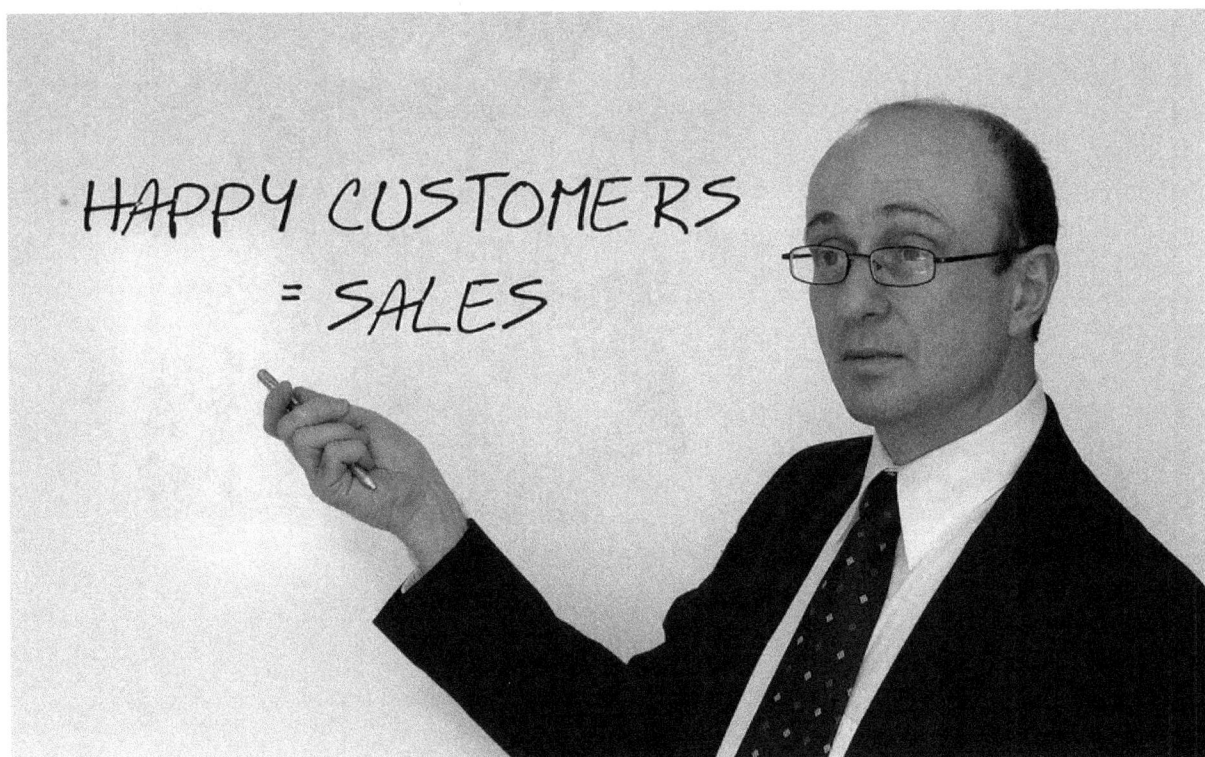

What is Prospecting?

Prospecting is a vital activity that every sales person must make a priority to do every day or week depending on the products/services you sell. In today's competitive environment, potential customers are not calling you and saying "Come see me so I can buy your product". One of the ways to find new customers is by strategically looking for them and there is no better tool to help to do that today than LinkedIn. LinkedIn is the only prospecting tool where you can find decision makers, learn about them both personally and professionally, and can even see a picture of them.

In this chapter, I am going to share with you how by using LinkedIn you can bypass the gatekeeper and get right to the decision maker.

You just have to look for customers sometimes....

10 Tips for Successful Prospecting

Statistics show that between 10to 15% of existing customers are looking for a new vendor and another 20 to 30% are willing to listen to a salesperson who can promise a better product or service. All you have to do is find the 20 to 30% that want to have a face to face meeting with you.

1. **Make an appointment with yourself for one hour each day to prospect.** Write the appointment into your smart phone, iPad, laptop or notepad – wherever you keep your calendar. You have to make this a priority. Prospecting should be placed on the same priority level as a meeting with a prospect or customer.

2. **If you set aside one hour a day for prospecting, make sure you focus on making calls.** It is usually a good idea not to take any phone calls during the hour you're devoting to prospecting. Distractions may dilute your results and keep you from committing to the full time.

3. **Make your calls brief.** The object of the prospecting is to get an appointment. Try to keep your call focused on introducing yourself and your product and getting an understanding of the prospect's needs. Provide the prospect with a good reason to meet with you.

4. **Be prepared with a list of names before you start making phone calls.** It is a great idea to always have a list of names and phone numbers you want to call in advance so you are not wasting time looking for this information when you should be making the phone calls. If for some reason you do not have the phone number of the decision maker, you can find this information by using sources like their company website, LinkedIn, Jigsaw, Google, and Manta just to name a few.

5. **Work without interruption.** The more often you prospect during a contiguous block of time, the better you become. Your second call will be better than your first, your third better than you're second, and so on.

6. **Prospect during off-peak hours instead of during conventional prospecting times.** The time of day you make your calls can have a major impact on your success. Prospecting early in the morning or late in the day can be very productive. Decision makers often work during off-peak hours.

7. **Vary your call times.** If you're told that a prospect is attending a meeting on Monday at 10 a.m., keep a log on each call, so you'll know when prospects aren't available. The key here is you must call back. You can never lose a sale until you decide to quit. If you're persistent, you'll notice a change of attitude in your prospects.

8. **Be organized.** Keep detailed records on each of your prospects, including notes on call information. When it comes to cold calling, the salesperson who keeps the best records usually wins.

9. **Envision the end before you begin.** Your goal is to get an appointment and your call should be designed to achieve that. Believe that your product and service will make the prospect better off.

10. **Don't stop at the close of the sale.** Persistence and follow through are the key virtues in selling success. Customers value stability in a sales person. They want to know that you will be there to help them implement the recommendations that you made.

PICK UP THE *phone* AND MAKE SOMETHING HAPPEN

Targeting Your Audience

I was talking to some successful small business owners about who the target audience is for their product/service. I was surprised that many of them had a difficult time clearly defining their ideal client. Understanding what verticals (industries) desire your product and services will allow you to have a laser-like focus.

Everything you do should be directed to the companies where your product/service will exceed requirements. The groups that you join on LinkedIn should be where your target audience is and you should be active in those groups so that the members begin to recognize you as the SME (Subject Matter Expert).

Strategies/Methods on Getting Face to Face Meetings

There are several ways to get an appointment with a decision maker. Let's examine a few of them.

Email: I have received so many emails from people trying to sell me on CRM platforms, websites, telemarketing, IT services, and many, many other products. There are several things all these emails had in common:

1. The email was too long.
2. They did not know anything about my company.
3. They sent two or more attachments.
4. They sent a generic email letter.
5. There was no call to action.
6. They never followed up with a telephone call.
7. Their email was about them and what they do.

Those are all things you ***should not do*** when attempting to get an appointment with the decision maker.

Here's What You Should Do:

1. Does some research on the company and decision maker before you send the email.
2. See if they have a company and/or a personal LinkedIn profile.
3. If they have a LinkedIn profile, read their entire profile for ideas on how to approach them.
4. See if you have any common connections. If you do, reach out to your common connection and ask them to introduce you to the prospect.
5. Design an introductory email letter that is short (100 words or less) and to the point about how you can help them solve their business' problems. Then, follow up a few days later with a phone call.

Here is a process I developed that I call being **"Pleasantly Persistent"** to help you get more appointments with decision makers:

1. Send introduction email – make sure you have a compelling subject line. It is important to note that we are intrigued by articles that have a headline that makes us want to read the article. Your subject line must have the same impact on your prospect.

2. Follow up with a phone call within 3 - 5 days.

3. Follow up email using the original introduction email. Hit "reply all" and say, "I am not sure you received my previous email so I'm re-sending." (Day 6-9).

4. Follow up with a phone call. (Day 10-12).

5. Send articles that are pertinent to your prospect.

6. Pay attention to what your prospect posts on LinkedIn and comment/like.

7. Send the prospect a unique/funny card.

Keep "**Pleasantly Pursing**" the prospect until you get a response. Then, develop your strategy for the next steps.

LinkedIn: This is probably one the best ways to get a meeting with a decision maker. Here are the steps:

1. Request a connection – make sure you include a personal note of why you want to connect with them. Do not be come across as a sales person because your request will be ignored.
2. Once they have accepted your request send them a" thank you" note stating you look forward to learning more about them.
3. Send a note stating that would like to have a brief chat with them to learn more about them. Suggest some date and times.

Phone Call:

1. Introduce yourself and set the agenda.
   Agenda: Mr. Jones, I would like to tell you about me and my company, learn about you and your situation, and lastly see if it would worth our time to meet.
2. Be prepared to handle a few objections (We 're all set, No budget, etc.)
3. Just have a conversation. (Do not give them a Sales Pitch.)

   Note: The goal of the phone call is to set up a face to face meeting. The longer you are on the phone the chances of you getting a face to face meeting drop dramatically. Get On and Get Off as quickly as possible.

Congratulations! You have a face to face meeting with a decision maker. Now what?

First Appointment Strategy

This is the most important meeting you will ever have with this decision maker. You need to bring your "A" game. Keep in mind you have spent several weeks, and sometimes months, trying to get the appointment with the decision maker, so don't blow it on the first meeting.

These are the six critical, qualifying questions every salesperson can benefit from asking.

1. **What needs does the prospect have that you can meet?**

   This question is even more important than whether the prospect is a decision maker. It is essential to clarify very early on whether the need for your product exists in any capacity. If not, you could be negotiating with the CEO and there'll still be no sale in the future.

2. **Does the prospect have the budget to purchase what you're selling?**

   The bigger the product or service, the less a small company can afford to purchase it. Even in a mid-size company, it's important to know how much money the prospect budgets for the service you're offering. You can get a feel for where the prospect's price range is by asking if they have a current vendor or if they've ever used services like yours in the past.

3. **When is the prospect looking to make a buying decision?**

   Salespeople sometimes spend months waiting while a prospect stalls. In a lot of cases, the prospect is contractually obligated to another supplier or is waiting for some other deadline to pass. It is good to know when the prospect is looking to make a buying decision. You can either save a lot of time and follow–up or create a timeline for the closing the sale. You can also work together to see if there's anything that can be done to expedite the process.

4. **Who will make the final decision?**

   In many cases, the final decision may not made by the person you're dealing with. A lot of decision makers expect their department heads to come to them with recommendations for major purchases. By knowing who makes the final decision, you can start to probe for more information about what factors influence the person's decision.

5. Who are the key players and do they influence the decision?

There are several periphery prospects in most buying decisions-end users, departmental personnel, and committee members. All of them play a crucial role in the decision-making process. Learning who they are and how the decision impacts them, helps you line up and prioritize your selling points. A benefit isn't a benefit unless it helps solve one of the prospect's problems.

6. Have you contacted more than one prospect in the company?

If there's more than one person who can benefit, it's in your best interest to speak to as many as possible. Tell your primary contact you want to gather more information so you can know which solution works best for them. Chances are each person can provide you with useful tips on how to sell to them. It's up to you to qualify each of them and move forward toward the sale.

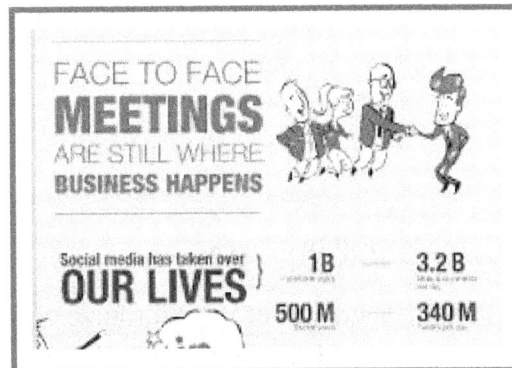

Close for the Next Step

The meeting is about to come to the end. Before you get up and leave, make sure you do the following:

1. **Summarize** the meeting and highlight the problem areas you uncovered from the prospect. Make sure the prospect is in agreement with the problem areas.

2. **Ask again** who is else would be involved in evaluating your products and services.

3. **Thank the prospect** for their time and being forth right about the company and their goals.

4. **Review the action** items and set up the next meeting.

The most important step that most sales people miss is that they do not schedule the next meeting with the prospect while they are there. What normally happens is the prospect says let's talk in a couple weeks. The sales person says, "Ok I will call you then." Then in two weeks the sales person calls and gets the prospect's voice mail. It takes another 2-3 weeks to reconnect with the prospect. This happened because the sales rep failed to get a specific date and time for the next meeting.

Here is what you should do:

Prospect: Let's get back together in two weeks.

Salesperson: Two weeks sounds great. Let's synchronize our calendars and pick a date and time that works for both of us. How about the 21st?

Prospect: Sure.

Salesperson: Great. Does morning or afternoons work best for you?

Prospect: Mornings.

Salesperson: Great .How about 10 a.m.?

Prospect: That works.

Salesperson: Here at your office?

Prospect: Yes.

Salesperson: What is the agenda for the meeting?

Prospect: Review pricing/implementation schedule.

Salesperson: Great. I will bring you a proposal with an implementation schedule. I will send you a meeting invite that way we can lock in the date and time we discussed.

Now you have a firm date, time and agenda for the next meeting. I guarantee that if you follow the steps above you will shorten your sales cycle and have more productive meetings. Always, Always, Always get a commitment from the prospect on specific date and time even if it's just to talk on the phone.

Be "Pleasantly Persistent" in acquiring new clients. Any questions?

Closing More Sales Today

As I reflect on what made my sales organizations successful over the years, I realized that one of the keys was that we simply closed more sales. So today I decided to share **5 ways that you can close more sales today**. As you read the 5 ways, you will find that these are things most of you are probably already doing today. But, I challenge each of you to ask yourself if you are consistently approaching each closing opportunity with a sense of urgency.

1. **Focus on preparation** – The more salespeople understand about the prospects and their companies, the stronger you can position your product/service as a viable alternative to solving their business needs thus creating a strong value proposition.

2. **Qualify up front** – You should have a set of qualifying questions in the cold calling process to quickly determine if this is a prospect or a suspect. It is critical that salespeople get the answers to those questions up front so they can determine what type of sales strategy will be required in the first face to face meeting.

3. **Become an industry expert** – In today's sales environment, sales people need to be viewed as a trusted consultant. Top sales people spend time learning all about their competition and are very versed on the latest industry trends. This is important because when the prospects ask questions about the competition or industry the salespeople can respond to those questions detailing why they should do business with their company or recommend another company.

4. **Develop a strong sense of empathy** – This is one of my favorite ways to close more sales. Top salespeople know that listening skills are the key to developing strong empathy. They ask a lot of open-ended questions at the beginning of the sales process which allows the prospect to do most of the talking. If you do not listen to what the prospect is saying you will not CLOSE MORE SALES.

5. **Maintain strong accountability** – Top salespeople are accountable to themselves and the customer they represent. Taking responsibility sends a strong message that the sales person can be trusted. When there is an issue/problem, the top sales person gets involved immediately and works diligently until the customer acknowledges that they are satisfied with the outcome.

Getting Prospects Excited About Doing Business with You

Selling Value comes down to one question:

<u>What can you provide that your competitors can't (or won't)?</u>

Salespeople who realize this are eager to learn everything they can about their prospects. The more avenues they go down, and the more they devote to understanding their prospect's needs, the stronger their selling points are.

Any salesperson knows that price is only one component of value. And really, what prospect wouldn't pay twice as much for a product that promised three-times the Return on Investment (ROI)?

So what becomes important throughout the selling process is maintaining focus on exactly what your company can provide to solve the prospect's biggest problem.

Prepping the Prospect and Yourself

First things first. You want a prospect to be excited about meeting with you. The more they're looking forward to it, the more inclined they'll be to give you their full attention.

That means when you get on the phone to call prospects, have your Smartphone, laptop, iPad, etc. calendar to book the appointment at the first available time and date. Sounds simple, right??

But the longer you've been at it, the easier it is to put the appointment off for a few days or perhaps a few weeks. Scheduling quickly keeps everything you talked about on the phone fresh in the prospect's mind, and it diminishes the chance they'll postpone or cancel the appointment.

Salespeople are well acquainted with the practice of sending promotional items, catalogs, or white papers to buyers. With email and overnight delivery, it makes it much easier to send information the prospect can review prior to the meeting.

Here are some examples you may have used to get the prospect engaged prior to the meeting with you, and provide them a chance to form questions of their own:

*A plain-English breakdown of any clinical research on your product, so the customer can understand what makes it superior.

*A list of ways your product/service can be used and how it can be used based on the company's need.

*A list of customer testimonials that focus on how the product/service has been effective, and/or

*A comprehensive list of product benefits, and additional services your company provides.

Selling Value at Game Time

It's what the voice in the back of very salesperson's head is saying to them before each presentation: Don't Oversell.

You want the prospect to expect great things from you, but you also want to promote a feeling of mutual trust and respect.

Here are some quick reminders of ways you can translate value and promote your company's reputation during the presentation:

*Handle objections head-on. Salespeople have heard every objection in the book. Over time, you create your own responses to each objection – answers that address the concern, place the prospects at ease, and bring the meeting back to the center.

*People do judge a book by its cover. It is unfortunate but true. Image is everything. There's an old exercise where you write down four words that describe how you want a prospect to view your company. Your appearance should reflect those four words.

*Ask pointed questions to uncover needs. A lot of salespeople are familiar with the phrase "perceived value". You may have the best benefit statement in the world. If they don't help fill the prospects' particular needs, they're useless.

Playing for the Long-Term

When a buyer signs on the dotted line, a sale ends and a relationship is born.

Potentially, that buyer could mean a great deal of repeat business. So it's wise to keep three loyalty-builders in mind:

A. **Resolve problems quickly and completely**.

B. **Maintain a regular follow-up schedule so nothing falls between the cracks**.

C. **Communicate each action to the customer. It helps to further establish trust**.

Final Thoughts

Most of you know finding new prospects is one of the most critical skills for sales professionals. In order to exceed your sales quota, you need quality prospects to move through the sales process. Like many of you, I am constantly seeking new business to achieve my sales goals. Develop the right attitude. Determination, perseverance, enthusiasm, and a positive attitude are the backbone of prospecting success. The correct mindset leads to successful prospecting and, ultimately, to more lucrative sales. Get positive, focused, and most of all, make it fun. Never stop looking for potential customers. Plan some time everyday to look for potential customers. Today's top salespeople recognize this and are using many different social media tools find new customers.

Find the real business issues facing your prospects. Every business has issues or needs. Experienced salespeople address those critical needs and link them to their products and services. You also want to target your prospects. Effective prospecting requires you to identify who your ideal customer is and how your product/service solves their business problem(s). You will find that is key to your overall progression. Once a prospect believes your message, the sale is made – even though the closing may take days or even months. Your knowledge moves the customer from prospect to customer so become an SME (Subject Matter Expert) in your field.

Once again, remember that once you identify a prospect, you need to find the decision maker. Who makes the decision? Is it a committee? Are their multiple levels required? It is critical to find this out, otherwise, you may end up meeting with people who cannot buy your product or service.

Congratulations! You are now armed and dangerous with simple and easy ways to close more sales today, tomorrow, and forever. Implement this repeatable process today and you will be on your way to closing more sales than you could ever imagine. No matter what you sell, remember it is always about the Customer and never about you. When you take care of the customer, the customer will take care of you.

ABOUT THE AUTHOR

Mr. Thomas Ellis is a results-oriented sales management veteran with over 30 years experience in coaching, consulting, and developing B2B sales professionals at all organizational levels. He enjoys the complete confidence of senior management, loyalty from sales teams, and respect from customers. A dynamic leader, Mr. Ellis specializes in driving rapid growth by forging strong relationships, and inspiring overachieving sales teams to work beyond their potential.

The training he offers does not over complicate the sales process and takes the mystery out of it by focusing on the fundamentals. The training focuses on:

Developing a Strategic Daily/Weekly Plan
Building Strong Relationships
Finding Great Prospects
Leveraging B2B Social Media to Get Warm Referrals
Conducting Effective Appointments
How to Overcome Objections and "Stalls"
Delivering Powerful Solution Presentations
How To Get Meetings with the Decision Makers
Negotiating and Closing the Sale
Effective Time Management Skills
Understanding and Demonstrating your Competitive Advantage
Uncovering the Needs of Your Prospects

Mr. Ellis is currently looking for sales teams, small business owners, and individual sales professionals who are ready to get more results this year, be successful mastering the basics and wants a proven sales winner to work with them step by step until they receive results!

There's no such thing as a successful golfer who doesn't have great form and can't make short putts; there is also no such thing as a successful sales person who hasn't mastered the basics of their profession! Mr. Ellis focuses on helping you master basic sales activities and small wins which leads to building your confidence and obtaining real success!

When you're ready to make every sales day count, please reach out to me for a FREE 30 minute consultation on how we can get started with a winning plan.

If Thomas is not out training clients on Sales Mastery or being a family man, you can find him indulging in his other true passion - Golf!

Contact Information

Website – www.ewcconsultants.com

Website – www.mrthomasellis.com

Twitter – MrThomasEllis

Skype – Thomasellis10

LinkedIn – http://www.linkedin.com/in/thomaseellis

Email – tellis@ewcconsultants.com

Phone – 301.343.0001

EWC CONSULTANTS
masters at developing sales teams

You can get anything you want in life if you just help enough other people get what they want.

Zig Ziglar

www.ingramcontent.com/pod-product-compliance
Lightning Source LLC
Chambersburg PA
CBHW051354200326

41521CB00014B/2577